Rewire Your Brain: A Practical Guide to Neuro-Linguistic Programming

Vipresh Dwivedi

DEDICATION

I wholeheartedly dedicate this book to all those courageous souls who find themselves facing struggles in their personal and professional lives. May this book serve as a guiding light, offering insights and tools to break free from repetitive patterns and fear of the unknown. May it inspire you to embrace change, learn from past experiences, and embark on a journey of growth and transformation. Remember, within you lies the strength to overcome any obstacles and create a life filled with joy, success, and fulfillment. You are capable of greatness.

Contents

ACKNOWLEDGMENTS

I am deeply grateful to Dr. Vandana, who guided me like an elder sister and taught me this technique after my brain stroke, helping me overcome depression. Special thanks to my friend, Dr. Papri, for constant motivation and visualization exercises during our everyday conversations, pushing me to believe in my recovery.

Chapter 1: The Foundations of Neuro-Linguistic Programming (NLP)

In this introductory chapter, we delve into the fundamental principles that form the bedrock of Neuro-Linguistic Programming (NLP). NLP is a powerful approach that explores the intricate connection between neurology, language, and behavior. We will uncover the origins of NLP, tracing its roots to the work of Richard Bandler and John Grinder in the 1970s. Understanding the structure of subjective experience and how individuals process information is key to NLP. We explore the concepts of representational systems, submodalities, and the impact of language on thought patterns. With a focus on sensory acuity and rapport-building techniques, you will gain insights into the transformative potential of NLP in personal growth, communication, and achieving desired outcomes.

•Understanding the origins and principles of NLP

Neuro-Linguistic Programming (NLP) traces its origins back to the early 1970s when it was developed by Richard Bandler and John Grinder. The duo studied successful therapists, such as Fritz Perls (Gestalt Therapy) and Virginia Satir (Family Systems Therapy), aiming to understand and replicate their effective techniques. They believed that by modeling the strategies of these experts, they could help others achieve similar positive results.

The principles of NLP are based on the idea that our experiences are subjective and shaped by how we process information through our senses. It emphasizes the profound connection between our neurology (brain and nervous system), language, and behavior. NLP proposes that individuals can reprogram their thought patterns and behaviors to achieve desired outcomes and overcome limiting beliefs.

The principles of NLP include:

Sensory Acuity: Being aware of and utilizing sensory information to understand oneself and others better.

Rapport Building: Establishing a deep connection with others by mirroring their non-verbal cues and creating a harmonious environment for effective communication.

Representational Systems: Recognizing that individuals use different senses to process information, such as visual, auditory, kinesthetic, olfactory, and gustatory, and tailoring communication accordingly.

Submodalities: Understanding the fine distinctions within sensory experiences and how they impact emotions and behaviors.

Anchoring: Associating specific stimuli with particular emotional states to access those states intentionally.

Reframing: Changing the way we interpret events or situations to alter our emotional responses and behaviors.

Modeling Excellence: Learning from successful individuals and emulating their strategies to achieve similar success.

Understanding and applying these principles can lead to personal growth, improved communication, and the attainment of desired outcomes in various aspects of life, making NLP a powerful tool for self-improvement and transformation.

•The connection between neurology, language, and behavior

The connection between neurology, language, and behavior is at the core of Neuro-Linguistic Programming (NLP). NLP posits that these three elements are deeply interlinked and influence each other in profound ways, shaping how individuals experience and interact with the world.

Neurology: The foundation of NLP lies in the belief that human experience is rooted in the neurological processes of the brain and nervous system. Our senses, such as sight, hearing, touch, taste, and smell, allow us to perceive the world around us. The brain processes this sensory information, and our mental representations of these experiences create our unique reality. NLP emphasizes that our neurological processes can be consciously managed and reprogrammed to achieve desired outcomes and overcome limitations.

Language: Language is not just a means of communication; it plays a pivotal role in shaping our thoughts, beliefs, and emotions. NLP focuses on the language patterns we use to represent and interpret our experiences. By paying attention to the words we choose, the metaphors we employ, and the way we structure our communication, NLP practitioners can gain insights into a person's thought processes and emotional states. Moreover, language can be used strategically to influence and inspire positive change in ourselves and others.

Behavior: Our neurology and language significantly impact our behavior. Our internal thought patterns, beliefs, and self-talk influence how we act in the external world. NLP recognizes that by understanding and modifying these internal processes, we can change our behaviors and responses to different situations. NLP techniques such as anchoring, reframing, and modeling aim to alter habitual patterns and empower individuals to respond more resourcefully to challenges.

In summary, NLP asserts that our neurology, language, and behavior are intimately connected. By gaining awareness of this connection and learning to harness its power, individuals can transform their lives, enhance communication, develop positive habits, and achieve personal and professional goals. Through NLP, people can create profound shifts in their mindset and behavior to live more fulfilling and successful lives.

•How NLP can create positive change and personal growth

Neuro-Linguistic Programming (NLP) offers powerful tools and techniques that can create positive change and foster personal growth in various aspects of life. Here are some ways in which NLP can facilitate positive transformations:

Overcoming Limiting Beliefs: NLP helps individuals identify and challenge limiting beliefs that hold them back from reaching their full potential. By reframing negative thought patterns and replacing them with empowering beliefs, NLP enables people to build self-confidence and take on new challenges.

Enhancing Communication Skills: NLP emphasizes effective communication, both with oneself and others. Through NLP techniques, individuals can improve their rapport-building abilities, active listening, and understanding non-verbal cues. This enhances their relationships and fosters better communication in personal and professional settings.

Managing Emotions: NLP provides tools to manage emotions constructively. Individuals learn how to regulate emotional responses, gain control over emotional triggers, and develop emotional resilience. This enables them to handle stress, anxiety, and challenging situations with greater ease.

Goal Setting and Achievement: NLP helps individuals set clear, achievable goals and develop action plans to reach them. By creating compelling visualizations and using techniques like "chunking down," people can break larger goals into smaller, manageable steps, making the path to success clearer and more attainable.

Overcoming Phobias and Fears: NLP offers techniques like "anchoring" and "swish patterns" to overcome phobias and fears. These methods help rewire negative associations and replace them with positive, empowering responses.

Modeling Excellence: NLP encourages modeling successful individuals who have achieved the desired outcomes. By studying and adopting the strategies and behaviors of these role models, individuals can improve their own performance and achieve similar success.

Enhancing Creativity and Problem-Solving: NLP fosters creativity by encouraging individuals to think outside the box and explore new perspectives. The ability to reframe problems and view them from different angles leads to innovative solutions and personal growth.

Building Resilience: NLP techniques help individuals build mental resilience by fostering a positive mindset and developing the ability to bounce back from setbacks and challenges.

Improving Self-Image: NLP helps individuals improve their self-image and self-esteem by enhancing their internal dialogue and cultivating a more positive self-concept.

Promoting Personal Alignment: NLP encourages individuals to align their values, beliefs, and actions to live a more authentic and purposeful life.

Overall, NLP is a versatile and transformative approach that empowers individuals to take charge of their lives, break free from limiting patterns, and unlock their full potential for personal growth and positive change.

Chapter 2: Building Rapport and Communication

In this chapter, we delve into the fundamental aspects of establishing meaningful connections with others. Rapport forms the cornerstone of effective communication, and this chapter explores various techniques to build rapport effortlessly. You will learn the art of active listening, understanding non-verbal cues, and mirroring body language to establish trust and foster deeper connections with people. The chapter also delves into the power of language and how to use language patterns effectively to influence and persuade others positively. Through practical exercises and real-life examples, you will gain invaluable insights into enhancing their communication skills and forging more authentic and harmonious relationships.

•Mastering the art of building rapport with others

Mastering the art of building rapport with others is a crucial skill that can significantly impact personal and professional relationships. Rapport is the foundation of effective communication, trust, and understanding, enabling individuals to connect with others on a deeper level. It plays a pivotal role in various aspects of life, from business negotiations to social interactions, making it a valuable skill to develop.

The first step in building rapport is to develop active listening skills. When engaging in a conversation, it's essential to focus fully on the speaker, showing genuine interest in what they are saying. Active listening involves giving your full attention, maintaining eye contact, nodding in agreement, and responding appropriately. By actively listening, you not only understand the speaker's words but also grasp their emotions and underlying messages.

Non-verbal cues are equally crucial in establishing rapport. Our body language communicates volumes about our thoughts and feelings. To build rapport, mirror the other person's body language to create a sense of familiarity and comfort. Subtle gestures like leaning forward when they do or matching their pace and tone of speech can create an unconscious connection between both parties.

Another effective way to build rapport is to find common ground. Discover shared interests, experiences, or beliefs that you can discuss. Shared experiences foster a sense of belonging and camaraderie, helping to bridge the gap between individuals and promoting a more profound understanding of each other.

Empathy and understanding are paramount in building rapport. Putting yourself in the other person's shoes allows you to appreciate their perspective and feelings. Show empathy by acknowledging their emotions and validating their experiences. Demonstrating genuine care and concern helps create a safe and trusting environment for open communication.

Furthermore, using positive and inclusive language enhances rapport-building efforts. Avoiding negative or judgmental language and instead, using affirmative words can encourage open and constructive discussions. Be respectful of the other person's ideas and opinions, even if they differ from your own.

In the digital age, building rapport extends to online interactions. Through virtual communication, maintaining eye contact is impossible, but active listening and attentive responses remain vital. Additionally, virtual rapport-building may involve acknowledging the challenges of the digital medium and being patient with potential delays or technical issues.

Mastering the art of building rapport with others is a multifaceted skill that requires practice, patience, and genuine interest in connecting with people. By developing active listening skills, being mindful of non-verbal cues, finding common ground, showing empathy, and using positive language, individuals can build strong and lasting connections with others. Whether in personal or professional settings, the ability to establish rapport enriches interactions, fosters mutual understanding, and lays the groundwork for fulfilling relationships.

•Enhancing your non-verbal communication skills

Enhancing your non-verbal communication skills is a powerful way to improve your overall communication effectiveness and create stronger connections with others. Non-verbal cues, such as body language, facial expressions, gestures, and tone of voice, play a significant role in conveying emotions, attitudes, and intentions. By being more conscious of and refining your non-verbal signals, you can make a positive impact on your personal and professional interactions.

Firstly, mastering body language is essential. Maintain an open posture with relaxed shoulders and arms to appear approachable and confident. Avoid crossing your arms or legs, as this can create a barrier between you and the other person. Make eye contact but remember to strike a balance; too little can make you seem disinterested, while excessive staring may feel uncomfortable.

Facial expressions are also key components of non-verbal communication. A warm and genuine smile can immediately put others at ease and convey friendliness and approachability. Be mindful of your facial expressions, ensuring they align with the emotions you wish to express during conversations.

Effective gestures can enhance your verbal communication and add emphasis to your points. Avoid fidgeting or making distracting movements, as they can convey nervousness or lack of confidence. Instead, use purposeful and controlled gestures to complement your words and engage your audience.

Tone of voice is another vital aspect of non-verbal communication. The way you speak can influence how your message is perceived. Aim for a clear and confident tone, and vary your pitch and pace to keep your audience engaged. Avoid speaking too loudly or softly, as it can create discomfort for others.

Cultural awareness is crucial when enhancing non-verbal communication skills. Different cultures may interpret body language and gestures differently, so being sensitive to cultural norms is essential to avoid misunderstandings. Educate yourself about the cultural practices of those you interact with regularly.

Self-awareness is a fundamental step in improving non-verbal communication. Pay attention to your own non-verbal cues and how they may impact others. Seek feedback from trusted friends or colleagues to identify areas for improvement.

Practicing active listening is a valuable complement to non-verbal communication. Demonstrate that you are fully engaged in the conversation by nodding, making verbal acknowledgments, and providing appropriate responses. Active listening shows that you value the other person's input and creates a positive communication environment.

Lastly, observe and learn from effective communicators around you. Pay attention to how they use their non-verbal cues to convey their messages and create meaningful connections. Emulate their techniques while still maintaining your authentic style.

Enhancing non-verbal communication skills is an ongoing process that can significantly improve your ability to connect with others and convey your messages effectively. By mastering body language, refining facial expressions and gestures, being mindful of your tone of voice, and considering cultural differences, you can become a more influential and persuasive communicator. Active listening and learning from skilled communicators further contribute to honing these skills and making a positive impact in both your personal and professional relationships.

•Utilizing language patterns for effective communication

Utilizing language patterns for effective communication is a powerful skill that can enhance your ability to influence and persuade others. Language patterns refer to the specific ways we structure our words and phrases to convey meaning, create rapport, and build understanding. By mastering various language patterns, you can become a more skilled communicator and achieve your desired outcomes in conversations, negotiations, and presentations.

One essential language pattern is the use of sensory language. Sensory language involves incorporating words that appeal to the five senses—sight, hearing, touch, taste, and smell—into your communication. By doing so, you can paint vivid mental images and evoke emotions in your listeners. For example, instead of saying, "The food was delicious," you could say, "The warm, flavorful dish melted in your mouth, leaving a lingering taste of spices." Sensory language allows your audience to better connect with your message and remember it more effectively.

Another valuable language pattern is the use of analogies and metaphors. Analogies and metaphors help explain complex ideas by relating them to familiar concepts. They make abstract concepts more tangible and accessible to your listeners. For instance, when describing a challenging project, you could say, "Navigating through that project was like solving a labyrinth, with new twists and turns at every corner." Analogies and metaphors add depth and richness to your communication, making it engaging and memorable.

The power of language patterns extends to using persuasive language. Employing persuasive language techniques can influence your audience's beliefs, attitudes, and actions. For example, using positive affirmations and strong, action-oriented words can inspire and motivate others. When presenting an idea, you could say, "By embracing this new approach, we will unleash our team's potential and achieve remarkable results."

Additionally, utilizing linguistic techniques such as presuppositions can subtly guide the direction of a conversation. Presuppositions are statements that assume the truth of certain elements. For instance, saying, "When you are ready to take the next step," presupposes that the person will indeed take that step. This technique can gently encourage others to consider the desired action as a natural progression.

Language patterns also include pacing and leading, a technique to establish rapport and create a sense of connection with your audience. Pacing involves mirroring or matching the language, tone, and body language of the person you're communicating with. Once rapport is established, you can lead the conversation in the direction you desire. Pacing and leading build trust and openness in a conversation.

Moreover, being aware of presuppositions and embedded commands can give your communication a subtle persuasive edge. These linguistic patterns involve embedding instructions within sentences to influence the listener's thoughts or behavior. For instance, "As you relax and consider this approach, you may find yourself becoming more open to change."

In conclusion, mastering language patterns is an invaluable skill for effective communication. Sensory language, analogies, persuasive language, presuppositions, pacing and leading, and embedded commands are powerful tools to engage, influence, and connect with others. By incorporating these language patterns into your communication style, you can enhance your ability to convey ideas, create rapport, and achieve your goals in various personal and professional settings.

Chapter 3: The Power of Subconscious Mind

This chapter, delve into the profound influence that the subconscious mind wields over our thoughts, behaviors, and overall well-being. This chapter explores the concept of the subconscious as a reservoir of beliefs, emotions, and memories that shape our daily experiences. You will gain insights into how the subconscious mind can be harnessed to facilitate personal growth, overcome limiting beliefs, and achieve desired outcomes. Techniques like visualization, affirmation, and reprogramming are covered, empowering you to tap into the immense potential of their subconscious minds to transform their lives positively and manifest their aspirations.

•Exploring the subconscious mind and its influence on behavior

The subconscious mind, a powerful and intricate aspect of our psyche, plays a profound role in shaping our behavior and experiences. While our conscious mind deals with logical thinking and decision-making, the subconscious operates silently beneath the surface, influencing our actions, emotions, and beliefs.

Understanding the subconscious mind requires recognizing its vast capacity to store memories, experiences, and emotions accumulated throughout our lives. It acts as a repository of our past, shaping our perceptions of the present and influencing our reactions to various situations. This reservoir of information affects how we interpret the world, make judgments, and respond to stimuli.

One of the most fascinating aspects of the subconscious mind is its ability to operate without our conscious awareness. It controls many automatic bodily functions, such as breathing, heartbeat, and digestion, ensuring our survival without requiring conscious effort. Additionally, the subconscious plays a crucial role in forming habits, allowing us to perform routine tasks effortlessly over time.

Our beliefs and attitudes are deeply influenced by the subconscious mind. Past experiences and societal conditioning can create ingrained thought patterns that impact our self-esteem, confidence, and overall worldview. If we hold negative beliefs about ourselves or the world around us, it can lead to self-sabotaging behaviors and limit our potential for growth.

However, the subconscious mind also offers an incredible opportunity for personal development and transformation. By gaining awareness of our deeply rooted beliefs and thought patterns, we can begin to challenge and reshape them. Techniques like visualization, meditation, and positive affirmations can help reprogram the subconscious, replacing limiting beliefs with empowering ones.

Moreover, exploring the subconscious mind can uncover the source of unresolved traumas or emotional wounds. Addressing these issues through therapy or self-reflection can lead to healing and greater emotional well-being.

NLP (Neuro-Linguistic Programming) is a powerful tool that enables individuals to delve into the workings of the subconscious mind and bring about positive change. By understanding the language and communication patterns of the subconscious, NLP practitioners can guide individuals towards overcoming phobias, changing undesirable behaviors, and achieving personal goals.

he subconscious mind is a profound force that significantly influences our thoughts, behaviors, and emotions. Its hidden power can either hinder our growth or be harnessed to facilitate positive change and personal development. Exploring the subconscious mind offers an exciting journey of self-discovery and transformation, paving the way for a more fulfilling and empowered life.

•Techniques to reprogram limiting beliefs and negative thought patterns

Reprogramming limiting beliefs and negative thought patterns is a transformative process that empowers individuals to break free from self-imposed limitations and live more fulfilling lives. These beliefs and thought patterns often originate from past experiences, childhood conditioning, or societal influences, and they can significantly impact our self-esteem, confidence, and overall well-being. Fortunately, various techniques can help us reprogram these limiting beliefs and replace them with empowering ones:

Self-Awareness: The first step in reprogramming limiting beliefs is becoming aware of them. Pay attention to your thoughts and identify patterns of negativity or self-doubt. Journaling can be a helpful tool to track and analyze these beliefs.

Cognitive Restructuring: Challenge and reframe negative thoughts. When you catch yourself thinking negatively, replace those thoughts with more positive and realistic ones. For example, if you believe you are not good enough, remind yourself of your past accomplishments and strengths.

Positive Affirmations: Create positive statements that counteract the limiting beliefs. Repeat these affirmations daily to reinforce new thought patterns in your subconscious mind. Affirmations like "I am capable," "I am worthy of success," or "I believe in myself" can be effective.

Visualization: Use the power of visualization to see yourself succeeding and overcoming challenges. Imagine yourself confidently handling situations that previously triggered negative beliefs. This practice helps create new neural pathways in the brain, reinforcing positive thinking.

Gratitude Practice: Cultivate gratitude for

what you have and who you are. Acknowledge your achievements and the positive aspects of your life, shifting the focus away from limiting beliefs.

Emotional Freedom Techniques (EFT): Emotional Freedom Techniques (EFT), commonly known as "tapping," is a powerful and holistic therapeutic approach that combines elements of traditional Chinese acupressure and modern psychology to address emotional and physical issues. Developed in the 1990s by Gary Craig, EFT aims to restore the balance of the body's energy system to promote emotional healing and overall well-being.

The foundation of EFT lies in the belief that negative emotions and traumatic experiences disrupt the body's energy flow, leading to emotional distress and physical ailments. By tapping on specific meridian points on the body while focusing on the emotional issue, EFT helps release energy blockages and restores equilibrium.

The technique is simple and can be practiced by anyone. It involves a series of gentle taps with the fingertips on acupressure points, such as the top of the head, eyebrows, side of the eye, under the eye, under the nose, chin, collarbone, and under the arm. While tapping, individuals also voice their feelings, thoughts, or memories associated with the problem.

EFT has shown remarkable effectiveness in reducing anxiety, stress, phobias, and traumatic memories. It is also used to alleviate physical pain and address negative thought patterns and limiting beliefs. By tapping on these points, individuals are thought to rewire their brain's responses to triggers and create new, healthier patterns.

Moreover, EFT is non-invasive, drug-free, and easy to learn. It can be self-administered or facilitated by a certified EFT practitioner. Many people find relief after just a few rounds of tapping, although deeper or more complex issues may require more extended practice or professional guidance.

While scientific research on EFT is ongoing, numerous studies and anecdotal evidence support its effectiveness in promoting emotional release, stress reduction, and improved emotional resilience. It is often used in conjunction with traditional therapy to enhance emotional processing and healing.

Hypnotherapy: Guided hypnosis can access the subconscious mind and implant positive suggestions, helping to reprogram limiting beliefs at a deeper level.

NLP Techniques: Neuro-Linguistic Programming offers various techniques like the "Swish Pattern," "Belief Change Pattern," or "Six-Step Reframe" to reprogram negative beliefs into positive ones.

Here's a basic overview of the Swish Pattern process:

1. *Identify the Unwanted Behavior or Trigger:* The first step is to clearly identify the specific behavior, habit, or emotional response that you want to change. This could be anything from a fear of public speaking to a tendency to procrastinate.

2. *Create the Desired Outcome:* Visualize the desired outcome or response you want to have instead of the unwanted behavior. Make the mental picture vivid and compelling, focusing on how you want to feel and act in that situation.

3. *Identify the Trigger Image:* Recall the mental image that represents the trigger for the unwanted behavior. This image typically precedes the unwanted response.

4. *Swish the Images:* In your mind, "swish" the unwanted image away quickly, like a sudden zoom-out or shrinking, and immediately replace it with the desired outcome image, which should be large, bright, and compelling. The swish should happen rapidly, like a snap or a blink.

5. *Repeat and Reinforce:* Practice the swish several times, making sure to focus on the positive outcome each time. The more you repeat the process, the more your mind reinforces the new pattern.

6. *Test and Refine:* Gradually expose yourself to the trigger in real-life situations, observing how your new response unfolds. If needed, refine the swish pattern to make it even more effective.

Mindfulness and Meditation: Practicing mindfulness helps observe thoughts without judgment, creating space to challenge negative beliefs. Meditation cultivates a calm and focused mind, reducing the influence of negative thought patterns.

Seek Professional Help: If limiting beliefs and negative thought patterns are deeply ingrained or causing significant distress, consider seeking help from a therapist or counselor. They can provide guidance, support, and tailored techniques to address your specific challenges.

Reprogramming limiting beliefs is a gradual process that requires patience and consistency. Embrace the journey of self-discovery and growth, and remember that with determination and the right techniques, you can transform your mindset and create a more positive and empowered life.

•Harnessing the subconscious for goal achievement

Harnessing the power of the subconscious mind is a key to unlocking our full potential and achieving our goals. Our subconscious mind plays a crucial role in shaping our thoughts, behaviors, and actions, and by aligning it with our conscious desires, we can supercharge our goal achievement process. Here's how to harness the subconscious for goal achievement:

Clear Goal Setting: Start by defining clear, specific, and achievable goals. The subconscious mind responds best to clear instructions, so be precise about what you want to achieve. Write down your goals to reinforce them in your mind.

Visualization: Use the power of visualization to see yourself accomplishing your goals. Create vivid mental images of successfully achieving each goal. Engage all your senses to make the experience more real, and feel the emotions associated with your achievements.

Positive Affirmations: Affirmations are powerful statements that declare your goals as already achieved. Repeat positive affirmations daily to program your subconscious mind with empowering beliefs. For example, say, "I am confident and capable of achieving my goals."

Repetition and Repetition: Repetition is the key to programming the subconscious mind. Continuously expose yourself to your goals and affirmations. Write them down, say them out loud, and visualize them regularly.

Emotional Alignment: Align your emotions with your goals. Cultivate a strong desire and passion for what you want to achieve. The stronger the emotional connection, the more powerful the impact on your subconscious.

Gratitude and Positivity: Practice gratitude for what you have and what you've achieved so far. Focus on the positive aspects of your journey, as a positive mindset enhances the receptivity of the subconscious.

Mindfulness and Self-Awareness: Stay mindful of your thoughts and self-aware of any negative beliefs or doubts that arise. When negative thoughts emerge, replace them with positive ones and recommit to your goals.

Embrace the Power of "I Am": The phrase "I am" has a profound effect on the subconscious. Be mindful of how you use "I am" in your self-talk. Avoid negative self-identifiers and embrace positive declarations.

Use the Law of Attraction: The Law of Attraction suggests that like attracts like. By focusing on positive thoughts and emotions related to your goals, you attract opportunities and resources that align with your desires.

Subliminal Messaging: Consider using subliminal messaging or audio recordings with positive affirmations that play while you work or relax. These messages bypass the conscious mind and directly influence the subconscious.

Celebrate Small Wins: Acknowledge and celebrate every small step you take toward your goals. Positive reinforcement enhances your belief in achieving larger goals.

Harnessing the subconscious for goal achievement requires consistency, patience, and belief in your abilities. As you work to reprogram your subconscious mind, you'll notice increased motivation, focus, and alignment with your goals. Remember, the subconscious mind is a powerful tool that, when harnessed effectively, can propel you toward success and personal growth.

Chapter 4: Anchoring and Emotional Management

This chapter, delves into the powerful techniques of NLP that help individuals manage their emotions and create positive associations with specific triggers or anchors. Anchoring involves connecting a particular stimulus with a specific emotional state, allowing one to access desired emotions when needed. This chapter explores various anchoring techniques, including how to establish and collapse anchors, thereby gaining control over one's emotional responses. You will learn how to replace negative emotional patterns with empowering ones, paving the way for emotional resilience and well-being. Through practical exercises and guidance, this chapter equips you with tools to master their emotions and lead more fulfilling lives.

•Utilizing anchoring techniques for emotional control

Utilizing anchoring techniques for emotional control is a fundamental aspect of Neuro-Linguistic Programming (NLP) that empowers individuals to manage their emotions effectively. Anchoring involves associating specific triggers or stimuli with particular emotional states. By establishing these anchors, individuals can access desired emotions at will, creating a sense of emotional control and stability in various situations.

To utilize anchoring for emotional control, one must first identify the emotions they wish to experience more frequently or access in specific circumstances. It could be confidence, calmness, motivation, or any other positive emotion. Next, they need to find a unique and distinct physical or sensory anchor to associate with that emotion. This anchor could be a touch, gesture, sound, or visualization.

For example, to anchor confidence, one could touch their thumb and index finger together. Over time, by consistently associating this anchor with the feeling of confidence, the mind creates a strong neural connection between the two. As a result, whenever the individual presses their thumb and index finger together in the future, it triggers the state of confidence.

Repetition and consistency are essential to reinforce the anchor's association with the desired emotion. Practicing the anchor in various contexts and emotional states strengthens its effectiveness. Additionally, anchoring works best when the desired emotional state is experienced at its peak intensity while establishing the anchor.

Apart from creating positive anchors, NLP also offers techniques to collapse negative anchors or disassociate undesirable emotions from specific triggers. This process involves reprogramming the mind's response to a previously negative stimulus by interrupting and reshaping the association.

Through anchoring, individuals gain the ability to regulate their emotions consciously. This newfound emotional control significantly impacts their behavior, decision-making, and overall well-being. Whether facing a challenging situation or striving to maintain a positive mindset, anchoring provides a reliable tool to influence emotional responses positively.

It's important to note that anchoring is a skill that requires practice and patience. NLP practitioners often work with trained coaches or therapists to refine their anchoring techniques and achieve desired emotional outcomes effectively.

Utilizing anchoring techniques for emotional control empowers individuals to shape their emotional experiences and responses. By associating specific triggers with desired emotions, NLP enables individuals to tap into positive states at will. Anchoring not only fosters emotional stability and resilience but also supports personal growth and improved relationships. With dedication and practice, anyone can harness the power of anchoring to lead a more fulfilling and emotionally balanced life.

•Managing stress and anxiety through NLP practices

Managing stress and anxiety through Neuro-Linguistic Programming (NLP) practices offers powerful tools and techniques to alleviate the emotional burden and regain a sense of calm and control. NLP recognizes that stress and anxiety are responses generated by our thoughts, beliefs, and perceptions about various situations. By understanding and reframing these patterns, individuals can effectively manage and reduce their stress levels.

One of the key NLP practices for stress management is "reframing." Reframing involves consciously shifting one's perspective on a particular situation to view it in a more positive or constructive light. By changing the way, we interpret events, we can alter our emotional response. For example, instead of seeing a challenging work project as overwhelming, reframing it as an opportunity for growth and learning can reduce stress and increase motivation.

Another essential NLP technique for stress management is "anchoring," which we discussed earlier. Anchoring can be applied specifically to manage anxiety and stress. Individuals can create a positive anchor associated with a state of relaxation or calmness. When feeling stressed or anxious, activating this anchor can help to induce a more relaxed state of mind and body.

Additionally, NLP offers "timeline therapy," a process that helps individuals release negative emotions and limiting beliefs associated with past events. Often, stress and anxiety are fueled by unresolved emotions from the past. Through timeline therapy, people can reframe and let go of these emotions, leading to a more peaceful and emotionally balanced present.

The use of language is another powerful aspect of NLP in managing stress and anxiety. By paying attention to our self-talk and using positive and empowering language, we can influence our emotional state positively. Replacing negative or self-critical thoughts with affirming and supportive language can reduce stress and foster self-confidence.

Moreover, NLP emphasizes the importance of setting clear and achievable goals. By defining specific objectives and breaking them down into smaller, manageable steps, individuals can create a sense of direction and purpose, reducing stress caused by feeling overwhelmed or directionless.

Breathing exercises and relaxation techniques are also integrated into NLP practices for stress management. By practicing deep breathing and mindfulness, individuals can lower their physiological stress responses and promote a state of relaxation.

Overall, NLP offers a comprehensive approach to managing stress and anxiety by addressing thought patterns, emotional responses, and behavioral strategies. Through reframing, anchoring, timeline therapy, language usage, goal setting, and relaxation techniques, individuals can transform their relationship with stress and anxiety. By incorporating these NLP practices into their daily lives, individuals can foster resilience, emotional well-being, and a greater sense of inner peace. However, it is essential to remember that NLP practices should complement professional medical advice and not replace it in cases of chronic or severe stress and anxiety.

•Building emotional resilience and self-confidence

Building emotional resilience and self-confidence are crucial aspects of personal growth and well-being, and Neuro-Linguistic Programming (NLP) provides powerful techniques to strengthen these attributes. Emotional resilience enables individuals to bounce back from adversity, cope with challenges, and maintain a positive outlook, while self-confidence empowers individuals to believe in their abilities and take on new opportunities with courage.

NLP offers various strategies to build emotional resilience. One such technique is "reframing," which involves changing the way we perceive and interpret events. By reframing challenges as opportunities for growth and learning, individuals can shift their mindset and build a more resilient attitude towards difficulties. NLP also emphasizes the importance of cultivating a growth mindset, believing that abilities can be developed through dedication and hard work, rather than seeing them as fixed traits. This mindset fosters resilience by encouraging individuals to view setbacks as temporary and solvable.

Moreover, NLP practices help individuals develop effective coping mechanisms for managing stress and emotional challenges. Through relaxation techniques, mindfulness, and self-regulation exercises, individuals can reduce the impact of negative emotions and maintain a sense of balance and control in challenging situations.

Another essential aspect of building emotional resilience is understanding and managing one's emotions. NLP provides tools for emotional intelligence, such as recognizing and expressing emotions in a healthy and constructive manner. By developing emotional awareness and regulation, individuals can respond more effectively to their emotions and prevent them from overwhelming their thoughts and actions.

In parallel with emotional resilience, NLP focuses on fostering self-confidence. Anchoring is a powerful NLP technique used to associate positive feelings and states with specific physical or mental cues. By anchoring feelings of confidence, individuals can access this resource whenever needed, helping them face challenges with assurance.

NLP also addresses limiting beliefs that hinder self-confidence. Through techniques like belief change or timeline therapy, individuals can identify and reframe negative beliefs about themselves and replace them with empowering ones. This transformation enhances self-confidence and self-image.

Additionally, NLP encourages setting well-defined goals and creating a roadmap to achieve them. By breaking down larger objectives into smaller, achievable steps, individuals can build momentum and celebrate each success, enhancing their belief in their capabilities.

Practicing positive self-talk is another key aspect of NLP for building self-confidence. By using affirmations and positive language, individuals can reinforce a more optimistic and self-assured internal dialogue.

In summary, NLP offers a comprehensive toolkit for building emotional resilience and self-confidence. Through reframing, coping strategies, emotional intelligence, anchoring, belief change, goal setting, and positive self-talk, individuals can cultivate inner strength and belief in their abilities. By regularly incorporating these NLP practices into their lives, individuals can develop a strong foundation of emotional resilience and self-confidence, enabling them to navigate life's challenges with grace and positivity.

Chapter 5: Modeling Excellence

This chapter delves into the process of modeling, wherein one studies the behaviors, beliefs, and strategies of high achievers in a particular field. By understanding the patterns that lead to their excellence, you can apply these insights to their own lives and endeavors. NLP provides a structured approach to modeling, allowing individuals to accelerate their growth and achieve remarkable results by adopting the proven practices and mindset of those who have already excelled in their chosen domain.

•Understanding the concept of modeling in NLP

Understanding the concept of modeling is a fundamental aspect of Neuro-Linguistic Programming (NLP). In NLP, modeling refers to the process of observing and replicating the behaviors, beliefs, strategies, and mindset of highly successful individuals or experts in a specific area to achieve similar outcomes. By studying and understanding the patterns of excellence displayed by these individuals, one can effectively learn from their experiences and apply their proven methods to their own lives and goals.

The concept of modeling in NLP is inspired by the idea that excellence leaves clues. Instead of reinventing the wheel, NLP practitioners seek to identify and adopt the successful patterns used by others to expedite their own growth and success. This can be applied to various domains, such as business, sports, communication, leadership, and personal development.

To begin the modeling process, one must select a suitable role model or exemplar who has achieved exceptional results in the chosen field. This individual serves as the source of inspiration and learning. NLP emphasizes the importance of selecting the right model, someone whose expertise aligns with the outcomes the learner seeks to achieve.

The next step is to observe the model's behaviors, actions, and responses closely. This involves not only external behaviors but also internal thought processes, beliefs, and emotional states. NLP practitioners use a variety of techniques to gain insight into the model's thought patterns and strategies.

The process of modeling goes beyond mere imitation. It requires an in-depth analysis and understanding of the underlying principles and components that contribute to the model's success. This includes exploring their beliefs, values, and self-image, as well as the strategies they use to overcome challenges and achieve their goals.

Once the key elements of the model's excellence are identified, the learner can begin to adopt and integrate these patterns into their own behavior and mindset. NLP provides various techniques and exercises to help individuals embody the successful patterns, effectively reprogramming their own minds to match those of the model.

As the learner practices and refines the modeled strategies, they gain mastery and competence in the chosen area. NLP encourages continuous refinement and adaptation, allowing individuals to tailor the learned patterns to their unique strengths and circumstances.

Overall, understanding the concept of modeling in NLP empowers individuals to learn from the best and leverage the wisdom of those who have already achieved greatness. It is a powerful tool for personal and professional growth, enabling individuals to realize their full potential and reach extraordinary levels of success.

•Learning from successful individuals and adopting their strategies

Learning from successful individuals and adopting their strategies is a key concept in personal development and growth. It involves studying the achievements and behaviors of accomplished individuals in various fields and applying their proven strategies to one's own life or endeavors.

This approach has been embraced by various disciplines, including Neuro-Linguistic Programming (NLP), as it offers valuable insights into how success can be achieved and replicated.

One of the primary reasons for learning from successful individuals is the belief that excellence leaves clues. By observing the patterns, habits, and decision-making processes of those who have achieved success, individuals can gain valuable knowledge and guidance for their own journeys. Successful individuals often embody qualities such as discipline, resilience, and innovative thinking, which can serve as powerful examples for aspiring achievers.

When adopting strategies from successful individuals, it is essential to identify role models whose achievements align with one's goals and values. Whether it is in business, sports, arts, or personal development, choosing the right role model ensures that the lessons learned are relevant and applicable. Role models can inspire and motivate individuals to aim higher and push their boundaries, while also serving as a source of guidance during challenging times.

To effectively learn from successful individuals, one must engage in active observation and analysis. This involves studying not only the outward behaviors and actions but also the mindset and thought processes that contributed to their success. Successful individuals often possess a growth mindset, determination, and the ability to overcome obstacles. Understanding and adopting these mental attributes can be as important as replicating their actions.

Learning from successful individuals does not mean blindly copying their strategies. Instead, it involves adapting and integrating these strategies to fit one's unique circumstances and strengths. Successful individuals provide valuable lessons that can be used as a foundation for personal growth, but it is crucial to personalize and tailor these insights to align with individual goals and aspirations.

In the context of NLP, the process of learning from successful individuals and adopting their strategies is known as modeling. NLP practitioners observe the behaviors, language patterns, and beliefs of experts in a particular area and use this information to develop effective strategies for their own growth and success. Modeling encourages individuals to explore the underlying principles behind success, fostering a deeper understanding of the strategies being employed.

Learning from successful individuals and adopting their strategies is a powerful approach to personal and professional development. It offers a roadmap to success by leveraging the wisdom and experience of those who have achieved greatness. Whether it is in the realm of business, sports, or personal growth, embracing the lessons of successful individuals empowers individuals to reach their full potential and create a path to excellence.

•Applying modeling techniques to improve performance in various areas

Applying modeling techniques to improve performance in various areas is a fundamental aspect of Neuro-Linguistic Programming (NLP). Modeling involves studying and emulating the behaviors, beliefs, and strategies of successful individuals or experts in a specific field to enhance one's own performance and achieve desired outcomes.

The first step in applying modeling techniques is to identify the area or skill in which improvement is sought. Whether it's excelling in public speaking, becoming a more effective leader, or mastering a particular sport, the process begins by selecting a role model who has achieved success in that domain. This role model serves as a source of inspiration and a reference point for understanding what is possible.

Once the role model is chosen, the focus shifts to observation and analysis. This involves closely studying the actions, language patterns, beliefs, and mental strategies of the expert. NLP practitioners pay attention to both the conscious and subconscious aspects of the role model's behavior, seeking to uncover the underlying principles and thought processes that contribute to their success.

As part of the modeling process, NLP practitioners aim to elicit the strategies employed by the expert. This involves breaking down the expert's skills and behaviors into specific steps or techniques that can be practiced and integrated into one's own repertoire. By deconstructing complex behaviors into manageable components, individuals can more easily grasp and apply these strategies to their own performance.

To effectively apply modeling techniques, it is essential to practice and internalize the identified strategies consistently. Repetition and deliberate practice are crucial in building new neural pathways and solidifying the skills being developed. As individuals apply the modeled strategies and techniques, they gradually move from conscious effort to unconscious competence, making the skills more natural and automatic.

Furthermore, feedback and self-awareness play a vital role in refining the application of modeling techniques. Constantly evaluating one's progress, receiving feedback from mentors or coaches, and making necessary adjustments are essential for continued growth and improvement. This feedback loop allows individuals to identify areas of strength and areas that require further development, leading to ongoing refinement of their skills.

It is important to note that modeling techniques can be applied to a wide range of areas, including business, sports, communication, leadership, and personal development. By studying and adopting successful patterns and strategies from various fields, individuals can benefit from a diverse range of insights and approaches to improve their performance holistically.

Applying modeling techniques in NLP is a

powerful and effective way to improve performance in various areas. By identifying successful role models, observing their behaviors and strategies, eliciting their skills, and practicing consistently, individuals can enhance their own performance and achieve exceptional results. The process of modeling empowers individuals to learn from the best, adapt proven strategies to their unique circumstances, and continuously refine their skills on the path to success.

Chapter 6: Strategies for Personal Transformation

This chapter delves into powerful tools and techniques within Neuro-Linguistic Programming (NLP) that facilitate profound personal growth and transformation. You will explore how to identify and break free from limiting beliefs and behavioral patterns. The chapter offers step-by-step guidance on setting compelling goals, creating an empowering vision for the future, and aligning the conscious and subconscious mind to achieve success. Through various NLP methodologies, such as timeline therapy, reframing, and parts integration, individuals can overcome challenges, heal emotional wounds, and cultivate a resilient mindset. This chapter empowers you to embark on a transformative journey towards a more fulfilled and empowered life.

•Discovering your values and aligning them with your goals

It is a crucial aspect of personal development and growth within Neuro-Linguistic Programming (NLP). Values are the core principles and beliefs that guide our decisions, behaviors, and perceptions of the world. Understanding and aligning our values with our goals is vital for creating a meaningful and fulfilling life.

NLP offers various techniques to uncover

and explore one's values. Through introspection and self-awareness exercises, individuals can identify the values that hold the most significance in their lives. These values could include love, success, creativity, honesty, compassion, freedom, or any other principles that resonate deeply with them.

Once the values are recognized, the next step is to align them with personal goals. When our objectives are congruent with our values, it creates a powerful driving force for achievement and fulfillment. For example, if someone values adventure and freedom, setting a goal to travel and explore new places aligns perfectly with their core values, motivating them to work towards it with enthusiasm.

Aligning values with goals also helps in overcoming obstacles and maintaining motivation during challenging times. When faced with difficulties, reminding oneself of the deeper reasons and values behind the goals can rekindle determination and perseverance.

Moreover, NLP techniques can aid in resolving conflicts that may arise when multiple values seem to compete. By understanding the hierarchy of values and their interplay, individuals can make more informed decisions that prioritize what truly matters to them.

Furthermore, NLP facilitates the transformation of limiting beliefs that might hinder aligning values with goals. Negative self-perceptions can be reframed, enabling a more empowering mindset to pursue and achieve aspirations.

This process of discovery and alignment leads to a sense of authenticity and congruence within oneself. When our goals are in harmony with our values, it enhances our overall well-being and satisfaction in life.

Discovering and aligning values with goals is an integral part of personal growth through NLP. By exploring the core principles that drive us and ensuring they align with our aspirations, we can pave the way for a more purposeful and rewarding journey towards success and fulfillment. NLP provides effective tools to understand ourselves better, eliminate self-imposed limitations, and create a life that truly reflects our deepest values and desires.

•Setting compelling outcomes and action plans for success

It is a crucial component of Neuro-Linguistic Programming (NLP) that empowers individuals to achieve their desired goals effectively and efficiently. It involves the process of defining clear and motivating objectives and creating actionable steps to turn these aspirations into reality.

The first step in this process is to establish compelling outcomes. These outcomes are the specific, well-defined, and inspiring goals that an individual wishes to achieve. NLP emphasizes the importance of formulating outcomes in positive terms, focusing on what one wants to achieve rather than what they want to avoid. A compelling outcome paints a vivid picture of the desired future, making it emotionally engaging and motivating.

NLP techniques, such as the "Well-Formed Outcome" model, aid in refining outcomes by ensuring they meet certain criteria. These criteria include being stated positively, being within one's control, being ecologically sound (meaning they do not negatively impact oneself or others), and being appropriately contextualized in time and space.

After defining compelling outcomes, the next step is to develop action plans. Action plans break down the larger goal into manageable and achievable steps. NLP techniques like the "Chunking Down" process help individuals identify the specific actions required to progress towards their outcomes. Breaking the journey into smaller, actionable tasks prevents overwhelming feelings and enables a focus on incremental progress.

Another essential aspect of creating effective action plans is to identify and utilize resources effectively. NLP encourages individuals to recognize and leverage their strengths, skills, knowledge, and support networks to facilitate goal achievement. Moreover, visualizing successful outcomes through techniques like "Mental Rehearsal" helps in building confidence and motivation to follow through with the action plans.

Throughout the process, NLP emphasizes the significance of flexibility and adaptability. Sometimes, circumstances change, and the original plan may need adjustment. NLP equips individuals with the ability to be agile and make necessary modifications to their action plans without losing sight of the ultimate outcome.

In addition to formulating action plans, NLP also addresses potential obstacles and challenges that may arise. By using techniques like "The Circle of Excellence" and "Reframing," individuals can manage fears, doubts, and negative thoughts that might hinder progress. They learn to shift their perspective and develop a more empowering mindset.

"Setting compelling outcomes and action plans for success" is a fundamental aspect of NLP that empowers individuals to achieve their goals effectively. By defining inspiring outcomes, breaking them down into actionable steps, and utilizing NLP techniques to overcome challenges, individuals can create a roadmap to success. NLP equips individuals with the necessary tools and mindset to navigate their journey, maintain motivation, and celebrate achievements on the path to realizing their aspirations.

•Using NLP techniques to overcome obstacles and achieve personal growth

It is a transformative process that empowers individuals to break free from limiting beliefs, negative thought patterns, and emotional barriers. NLP offers a versatile set of tools and strategies that facilitate self-discovery, personal development, and ultimately, the achievement of one's full potential.

1. One of the key NLP techniques for overcoming obstacles is "*Reframing*."

Reframing involves changing the way an individual perceives a situation or challenge. By altering the meaning attached to an experience, individuals can shift from a negative perspective to a more empowering and positive one. This technique helps individuals view obstacles as opportunities for growth and learning, leading to increased resilience and problem-solving abilities.

2. Another powerful NLP tool is "*Anchoring*." Anchoring enables individuals to create positive emotional states and associate them with specific triggers. By recalling these positive states when facing obstacles, individuals can access a heightened sense of confidence, motivation, and resourcefulness. This technique helps in maintaining a positive mindset even during

challenging situations.

3. Furthermore, NLP offers techniques like "*Timeline Therapy*" to address past traumas and emotional baggage that may hinder personal growth. By revisiting past memories and reframing negative emotions associated with them, individuals can release emotional blocks and achieve emotional freedom. This process allows them to move forward with a renewed sense of purpose and clarity.

The process of Timeline Therapy typically involves the following steps:

Accessing the Timeline: The individual is guided into a relaxed and focused state, often referred to as an "associated" state, where they can access their subconscious mind and memories more readily. From this state, they can mentally visualize their timeline, which may appear as a line, a pathway, or even a series of connected images.

Releasing Negative Emotions: Once the timeline is accessible, the individual is guided to pinpoint specific events from their past that are associated with negative emotions or unresolved issues. These emotions could include anger, sadness, fear, guilt, or any other negative feelings. Through the guidance of a trained practitioner, the person releases and clears these negative emotions associated with the events.

Eliminating Limiting Beliefs: In addition to releasing negative emotions, Timeline Therapy helps identify and eliminate limiting beliefs that may have developed as a result of past experiences. These beliefs could be holding the individual back from achieving their goals and living a fulfilling life. The process involves recognizing the limiting beliefs, understanding their origins, and transforming them into positive and empowering beliefs.

Creating a Compelling Future: Once the past issues are resolved, the individual is guided to create a positive and compelling vision for their future. By mentally projecting themselves into the future and visualizing their desired outcomes, they can align their subconscious mind with their goals and aspirations.

4. Moreover, "*Parts Integration*" is an NLP technique that assists individuals in resolving internal conflicts. Often, conflicting parts of one's personality can impede personal growth and decision-making. Through Parts Integration, individuals can harmonize these conflicting aspects, aligning them with their core values and goals, and achieve greater inner

harmony and focus.

The process of Parts Integration typically involves the following steps:

Identifying Conflicting Parts: The individual is guided to identify the conflicting parts within themselves by exploring their internal dialogue, emotions, and beliefs. This step aims to bring awareness to the different aspects that contribute to their internal conflict.

Understanding the Positive Intent: Each part is recognized for having a positive intent or purpose, even if their strategies and behaviors may seem conflicting. This step involves exploring the underlying motivations and benefits of each part's perspective.

Negotiating Alignment: The conflicting parts are invited to enter into a dialogue facilitated by the practitioner or individual themselves. The purpose of this dialogue is to find common ground, understand each part's concerns, and negotiate a resolution that serves the overall well-being and highest intent of the person.

Integration: Once an agreement or alignment is reached, the conflicting parts are integrated into a unified state. This integration involves bringing the positive intentions of each part into alignment and creating a cohesive and integrated state of being.

5. NLP also emphasizes the importance of setting well-defined goals and adopting effective strategies for goal achievement. By applying techniques like "*The Disney Strategy*," individuals can generate creative ideas and action plans to overcome obstacles and reach their objectives. This approach encourages a balance

between innovative thinking and practical implementation.

The Disney Strategy is an NLP (Neuro-Linguistic Programming) technique that helps individuals enhance their creativity and problem-solving abilities by adopting three distinct thinking styles, each named after a different role associated with Walt Disney. The technique is inspired by Walt Disney's unique approach to creativity, where he would wear three metaphorical hats, representing different perspectives, to tackle a challenge or develop new ideas. These three thinking styles are commonly referred to as the Dreamer, the Realist, and the Critic.

The Dreamer: The Dreamer thinking style is all about free and imaginative thinking. During this phase, individuals unleash their creativity and let their minds wander without any limitations. They ask themselves, "What would be the ideal outcome? What are the wildest possibilities?" This part of the strategy allows individuals to generate innovative and unconventional ideas without being constrained by practicalities or limitations.

The Realist: After the Dreamer phase, individuals switch to the Realist thinking style. Here, they take a more pragmatic approach and analyze the ideas generated in the Dreamer phase. They ask themselves, "What resources do we have? What are the practical steps to achieve the ideas?" The Realist brings a sense of grounding and feasibility to the creative process, evaluating the potential challenges and planning the necessary steps to turn ideas into reality.

The Critic: The third and final thinking style in the Disney Strategy is the Critic. In this phase, individuals objectively assess and critique the ideas and plans developed in the Realist phase. They ask themselves,

"What potential issues or drawbacks might arise? How can we improve the ideas further?" The Critic helps identify potential pitfalls and refines the plans to make them more robust and effective.

The key to effectively using the Disney Strategy is to separate these three thinking styles distinctly. During each phase, individuals fully immerse themselves in the mindset of the specific role, preventing any crossover or interference between the roles. By doing so, individuals can prevent premature judgment and allow for a more comprehensive exploration of ideas.

By utilizing the Disney Strategy, individuals can gain a holistic perspective when approaching challenges or creative endeavors. It encourages the integration of creativity, practicality, and critical thinking, leading to well-rounded and innovative solutions. This technique is often employed in various fields, such as product development, problem-solving sessions, creative brainstorming, and project planning, to stimulate creativity and uncover innovative solutions to complex problems.

6. Additionally, "*Submodalities*" are an essential aspect of NLP that enables individuals to reprogram their thought patterns. By exploring the sensory qualities of thoughts, such as images, sounds, and feelings, individuals can modify the intensity and impact of their beliefs. This technique helps in transforming self-limiting beliefs into empowering beliefs that support personal growth and success.

In Neuro-Linguistic Programming (NLP), "Submodalities" refer to the finer distinctions within our sensory experiences that shape how we perceive and process information. Our five senses - visual (sight), auditory (sound), kinesthetic (touch), olfactory (smell), and gustatory (taste) - are not uniform experiences; they consist of various submodalities that can be manipulated to change our subjective experiences and responses to stimuli.

NLP practitioners use the concept of submodalities to understand how individuals encode and represent their experiences in their minds. By identifying and modifying these submodalities, NLP aims to help individuals overcome limitations, change unhelpful thought patterns, and enhance positive emotions and behaviors.

Some common submodalities include:

Visual Submodalities: Within the visual sense, submodalities involve aspects such as brightness, size, color, clarity, and distance. For example, if someone has a negative memory, reducing the brightness or size of the mental image associated with that memory can help decrease its emotional impact.

Auditory Submodalities: Within the auditory sense, submodalities include volume, pitch, speed, and location. Altering the volume or speed of an internal dialogue can influence how a person perceives and responds to self-talk.

Kinesthetic Submodalities: In the kinesthetic sense, submodalities involve factors like temperature, pressure, texture, and movement. Changing the way we internally experience sensations can impact our emotional responses.

Olfactory and Gustatory Submodalities: Submodalities for smell and taste might include intensity, quality, and association. These submodalities can be relevant in areas such as managing cravings or enhancing positive associations.

By understanding the role of submodalities in shaping our mental experiences, NLP practitioners can employ various techniques to create positive changes. For instance, the "Swish Pattern" aims to replace negative associations with positive ones by modifying the submodalities of specific mental images.

Additionally, NLP uses submodalities in techniques like "Fast Phobia Cure" to help individuals overcome phobias or anxieties by altering the sensory representations of the feared object or situation.

Ultimately, NLP provides a holistic approach to overcoming obstacles and achieving personal growth. By combining powerful techniques for reframing, anchoring, timeline therapy, parts integration, goal setting, and submodalities, individuals can develop a growth mindset, build emotional resilience, and unlock their full potential. NLP empowers individuals to take charge of their lives, embrace change, and create positive transformations that lead to lasting personal growth and fulfillment.

Chapter 7: NLP in Relationships

This chapter deals into the profound impact of Neuro-Linguistic Programming on fostering healthy and fulfilling connections with others. This chapter explores how NLP techniques can enhance communication, empathy, and understanding within various relationships, including romantic partnerships, family dynamics, friendships, and professional interactions. You will discover practical tools to improve active listening, resolve conflicts amicably, and build rapport effortlessly. By applying NLP principles, individuals can strengthen emotional bonds, cultivate mutual respect, and navigate the complexities of human connections with greater harmony and authenticity. This chapter empowers you to transform your relationships positively and create more meaningful and gratifying connections with the people in their lives.

•Enhancing communication and understanding in personal relationships

This is a pivotal chapter that explores how Neuro-Linguistic Programming (NLP) can profoundly improve the way we interact with our loved ones, fostering deeper connections and nurturing healthier relationships. Effective communication is the cornerstone of any successful relationship, and NLP provides valuable tools and techniques to enhance this crucial aspect.

NLP emphasizes the importance of active listening and understanding the underlying emotions and needs behind verbal and non-verbal cues. By practicing active listening, individuals can create a safe and supportive space for their partners, family members, and friends to express themselves authentically and without judgment.

One fundamental concept in NLP is representing the world through different representational systems, namely visual, auditory, kinesthetic, olfactory, and gustatory. Understanding the dominant representational system of our partners and loved ones helps tailor our communication style to resonate better with them, deepening mutual understanding.

Another essential aspect of NLP in relationships is perceptual positions. This technique allows individuals to view situations from different perspectives, such as their own, their partner's, and that of a neutral observer. By adopting these various viewpoints, one gains insight into the other person's emotions, thoughts, and motivations, fostering empathy and reducing conflicts.

NLP also explores the significance of language patterns and the impact of words on our relationships. Learning to use positive and empowering language can create a more nurturing and loving atmosphere, while avoiding negative and accusatory language helps prevent misunderstandings and hurt feelings.

Furthermore, the role of values and beliefs in relationships. Identifying shared values and aligning them with relationship goals can bring couples closer and create a stronger bond. Conversely, recognizing and addressing conflicting values can prevent potential issues from escalating.

In addition to enhancing communication, NLP provides powerful techniques to manage and resolve conflicts constructively. By using techniques such as reframing, where negative perceptions are transformed into positive ones, couples can shift their perspective and find mutually beneficial solutions.

•Resolving conflicts and building stronger connections

Resolving Conflicts and Building Stronger Connections is a crucial aspect of utilizing Neuro-Linguistic Programming (NLP) to foster healthier relationships. Conflict is a natural part of any relationship, but how we handle and resolve it can significantly impact the quality and longevity of our connections with others.

NLP offers a range of techniques to address conflicts effectively and strengthen the bond between individuals. One such technique is reframing, which involves changing the way we perceive and interpret a situation. By viewing conflicts as opportunities for growth and learning, rather than as obstacles, we can approach them with a more positive and constructive mindset.

Active listening plays a vital role in resolving conflicts. NLP emphasizes the importance of being fully present and attentive when engaging in discussions with our partners or loved ones. By actively listening and understanding each other's perspectives, we can bridge gaps in communication and find common ground.

Another powerful NLP technique for conflict resolution is using perceptual positions. This involves stepping into the shoes of the other person and seeing the situation from their perspective. By gaining insights into their emotions and motivations, we can develop empathy and a deeper understanding of their needs and concerns.

NLP also emphasizes the importance of using "I" statements instead of "you" statements when expressing feelings or concerns. This helps avoid blame and defensiveness, creating a safer space for open and honest communication.

Building rapport is another critical aspect of resolving conflicts and strengthening connections. NLP techniques can help individuals establish rapport with their partners by mirroring their body language, tone of voice, and language patterns. When done genuinely, mirroring fosters a sense of trust and connection between the parties involved.

Anchoring is yet another powerful NLP tool that can help manage conflicts. By associating positive emotions with specific gestures or words, individuals can use anchors to de-escalate tense situations and create a more positive and relaxed atmosphere.

NLP also explores the role of values and beliefs in conflicts. By identifying and understanding the values and beliefs driving each party's actions, individuals can find common ground and work towards mutually agreeable solutions.

NLP techniques empowers individuals to navigate conflicts with greater understanding, empathy, and communication. By embracing conflicts as opportunities for growth and learning, and by using techniques such as reframing, active listening, perceptual positions, and anchoring, individuals can create more profound and harmonious connections with their partners and loved ones. The result is not only the resolution of conflicts but also the strengthening of the emotional bonds that underpin healthy and fulfilling relationships.

•Empowering yourself and others to thrive in relationships

It is a pivotal aspect of utilizing Neuro-

Linguistic Programming (NLP) principles to cultivate strong, fulfilling, and harmonious connections with others. NLP offers a range of empowering techniques that enable individuals to foster healthy relationships and create positive impacts on those around them.

One of the key elements of empowering oneself in relationships is by developing self-awareness. NLP emphasizes the importance of understanding one's emotions, beliefs, and communication patterns. By gaining insight into our own behaviors and thought processes, we can identify areas for personal growth and take responsibility for our actions within relationships.

Empowering oneself also involves setting healthy boundaries. NLP teaches individuals to assert their needs and communicate their boundaries clearly and confidently. This enhances self-respect and garners respect from others, leading to more balanced and respectful relationships.

In addition to self-empowerment, NLP provides tools to empower others in relationships. One such technique is "embedded commands," where individuals subtly suggest empowering ideas to others within their language patterns. This can influence the mindset of the other person positively and encourage them to adopt a more empowered perspective.

NLP also highlights the significance of understanding love languages, which are the unique ways individuals express and interpret love. By recognizing and catering to each other's love languages, partners can strengthen their emotional connection and foster a more intimate and satisfying relationship.

Embedded commands typically involve using specific language patterns to make certain words or phrases stand out subtly.

These words are often spoken with a slightly different tone, volume, or emphasis, which signals the subconscious mind to pay closer attention to them.

For example, consider the following sentence:

"You can relax your mind and begin to feel more confident."

In this sentence, the embedded command is "relax your mind" and "feel more confident." The word "relax" is emphasized to subtly suggest to the listener to relax their mind, and "feel more confident" is structured as a suggestion rather than a direct command.

Another empowering aspect of NLP is fostering a growth mindset in relationships. This involves viewing challenges as opportunities for growth and believing that relationships can evolve positively over time. A growth mindset encourages continuous learning, adaptability, and resilience, leading to stronger and more dynamic connections.

Empowering communication is an essential component of thriving relationships. NLP techniques such as active listening, using "I" statements, and employing non-judgmental language foster an environment of openness and understanding. This creates a safe space for honest expression and emotional vulnerability, further deepening the bond between individuals.

Moreover, NLP enables individuals to recognize and reframe limiting beliefs that may hinder relationship growth. By challenging and replacing these negative beliefs with empowering ones, individuals can experience more enriching and rewarding relationships.

Lastly, empowering oneself and others in relationships involves the practice of appreciation and gratitude. NLP encourages individuals to express gratitude and acknowledge the positive qualities of their partners regularly. This reinforces feelings of love and connection and fosters a supportive and uplifting relationship dynamic.

In conclusion, "Empowering Yourself and Others to Thrive in Relationships" through NLP principles empowers individuals to take charge of their emotional well-being and communication patterns. By fostering self-awareness, setting healthy boundaries, and adopting a growth mindset, individuals can cultivate stronger and more fulfilling relationships. The use of empowering language, understanding love languages, and promoting gratitude further enhances emotional connections with others. Through NLP, individuals can create a positive ripple effect in their relationships, leading to increased happiness, trust, and mutual growth.

Chapter 8: NLP in Business and Leadership

In this chapter we explore the transformative application of Neuro-Linguistic Programming (NLP) principles in the corporate world and leadership roles. This chapter delves into how NLP techniques can enhance communication, negotiation skills, and conflict resolution in business settings. It highlights the importance of building rapport with clients, employees, and stakeholders to foster successful collaborations. Moreover, the chapter showcases how NLP can empower leaders to inspire and motivate their teams effectively. By mastering NLP strategies, individuals in business and leadership positions can elevate their performance, drive innovation, and create a positive and thriving work environment.

•Applying NLP techniques for effective leadership

Applying Neuro-Linguistic Programming (NLP) techniques for effective leadership can be a transformative and empowering experience. NLP provides leaders with valuable tools to enhance their communication, influence, and decision-making skills, enabling them to inspire and motivate their teams effectively.

One crucial aspect of NLP in leadership is understanding and building rapport with team members. By using non-verbal cues and language patterns, leaders can create a sense of trust and connection with their employees. This fosters a positive and supportive work environment, where team members feel valued and understood.

Another key NLP technique for leadership is modeling excellence. Leaders can study and emulate the behaviors and strategies of successful individuals in their field, learning from their best practices. By adopting these successful patterns, leaders can improve their own performance and guide their teams towards achieving outstanding results.

NLP also offers techniques for setting compelling outcomes and action plans. Effective leaders know how to set clear and inspiring goals for themselves and their teams. They create actionable plans, breaking down larger objectives into manageable steps, and provide continuous feedback and support to ensure progress and success.

In addition to goal setting, NLP helps leaders overcome obstacles and challenges that may arise. Through techniques like reframing and anchoring, leaders can change their perspective on difficult situations, turning setbacks into learning opportunities and finding solutions to problems more effectively.

Furthermore, NLP enhances a leader's emotional intelligence. Leaders who can manage their emotions and understand the emotions of others can create a positive and motivating work atmosphere. This emotional awareness allows leaders to address conflicts and difficult conversations with empathy and sensitivity.

Leadership presence is another area that benefits from NLP techniques. By improving their communication and body language, leaders can exude confidence and authority, gaining the trust and respect of their teams.

Effective delegation is a crucial skill for leaders, and NLP can assist in this aspect as well. By understanding the preferred communication styles and strengths of team members, leaders can delegate tasks more efficiently, ensuring that each individual can contribute their best to the team's overall success.

In summary, applying NLP techniques for effective leadership empowers leaders to build strong relationships, set compelling goals, overcome challenges, and foster a positive and productive work environment. By harnessing the power of NLP, leaders can unlock their full potential and inspire their teams to achieve greatness together.

•Improving communication and negotiation skills in the business environment

Improving communication and negotiation skills in the business environment is essential for success in today's competitive world. Utilizing Neuro-Linguistic Programming (NLP) techniques can significantly enhance these skills, leading to more effective interactions and positive outcomes.

NLP emphasizes the importance of building rapport and understanding the communication styles of others. By becoming attuned to verbal and non-verbal cues, professionals can establish trust and create a conducive environment for open dialogue. Active listening, mirroring, and matching techniques enable individuals to connect better with colleagues, clients, and partners, fostering strong relationships.

One of the cornerstones of NLP for communication is using language patterns to influence and persuade. Employing persuasive language, such as using "you" instead of "I" statements, helps individuals articulate their ideas more effectively. Additionally, NLP teaches professionals to be flexible in their communication, adjusting their language and approach to suit the preferences and personalities of different individuals.

Negotiation is a vital aspect of the business environment, and NLP equips individuals with powerful tools to improve negotiation skills. Understanding and managing one's emotions during negotiations is key to maintaining composure and making rational decisions. NLP techniques, like anchoring positive states, help individuals stay focused and confident during high-stakes negotiations.

Furthermore, NLP teaches professionals to

adopt a win-win mindset in negotiations, seeking mutually beneficial outcomes. By actively listening and understanding the interests and needs of the other party, negotiators can identify common ground and propose solutions that satisfy both sides.

Building rapport is equally crucial during negotiations. NLP techniques allow individuals to establish rapport quickly, creating a positive atmosphere that fosters collaboration and productive problem-solving. Employing body language mirroring and pacing, negotiators can establish trust and understanding with the other party.

NLP also helps professionals manage objections and navigate challenging situations during negotiations. Through reframing techniques, individuals can turn objections into opportunities for constructive dialogue, ultimately leading to more favorable outcomes.

Visualization is another powerful NLP tool for improving communication and negotiation skills. By mentally rehearsing important conversations or negotiation scenarios, individuals can boost their confidence and increase their chances of success.

Improving communication and negotiation skills in the business environment through NLP techniques can lead to more effective interactions, enhanced relationships, and successful outcomes. By focusing on building rapport, utilizing persuasive language patterns, managing emotions, and adopting a win-win mindset, professionals can excel in their communication and negotiation endeavors, contributing to their personal and organizational growth and success.

•Enhancing team performance and fostering a positive organizational culture

Enhancing team performance and fostering a positive organizational culture are vital aspects of creating a thriving and successful business. Neuro-Linguistic Programming (NLP) offers valuable tools and techniques that can significantly impact team dynamics, communication, and overall performance.

One of the fundamental principles of NLP is the understanding that each individual has a unique perspective and preferred communication style. By recognizing and respecting these differences, team members can build stronger connections and collaborate more effectively. NLP encourages open and honest communication, where team members actively listen to each other's ideas and opinions without judgment.

NLP also emphasizes the importance of setting clear and compelling goals for the team. When everyone understands the common objectives and their role in achieving them, it fosters a sense of purpose and motivation. Utilizing NLP techniques like outcome setting and visualization, teams can align their efforts towards shared success.

Building rapport within the team is essential for creating a positive and supportive work environment. NLP provides practical tools for enhancing rapport, such as mirroring and matching body language, tone of voice, and language patterns. This fosters trust and a sense of camaraderie among team members, leading to increased collaboration and synergy.

NLP techniques can also be employed to manage conflicts and address challenges within the team constructively. Through reframing and reevaluating situations from different perspectives, team members can find common ground and reach mutually beneficial solutions. NLP also encourages individuals to take responsibility for their emotions and responses, promoting a culture of accountability and respect.

A positive organizational culture is built on effective leadership, which is another area where NLP can make a significant impact. NLP-based leadership emphasizes leading by example, building strong relationships with team members, and empowering them to reach their full potential. NLP techniques, such as anchoring positive emotions and effective feedback, enable leaders to inspire and motivate their teams.

Encouraging a growth mindset within the organization is also essential for enhancing team performance. NLP principles emphasize the idea of continuous learning and improvement. Leaders can use NLP techniques to instill a culture of curiosity, adaptability, and innovation within their teams.

To foster a positive organizational culture, NLP can also be applied to improve employee engagement and satisfaction. By understanding individual values and aligning them with the organization's mission, leaders can create a sense of purpose and fulfillment among employees. NLP techniques, like goal-setting and reframing limiting beliefs, can help employees overcome challenges and stay focused on their personal and professional growth.

By incorporating NLP principles and techniques, organizations can enhance team performance, communication, and collaboration. Fostering a positive organizational culture that values individual differences, promotes open communication, and encourages continuous learning can lead to increased employee engagement, improved productivity, and overall business success. NLP provides a holistic approach to empower teams and leaders, making it a valuable tool for creating thriving workplaces.

Chapter 9: Overcoming Challenges and Fears

In this chapter, we delve into the powerful application of Neuro-Linguistic Programming (NLP) techniques to address and conquer personal obstacles. This chapter offers insights into understanding the root causes of fears and challenges that hold individuals back. By employing various NLP methods like reframing limiting beliefs, visualization, and anchoring positive emotions, you can develop resilience and transform your mindset. From managing anxiety to breaking free from self-imposed limitations, this chapter provides practical strategies to build inner strength, embrace change, and navigate life's hurdles with confidence and determination. Empowering you to face challenges head-on, it paves the way for a more fulfilling and enriching journey ahead.

•Strategies to overcome fears, phobias, and limiting beliefs

In the realm of Neuro-Linguistic Programming (NLP), empowering individuals to overcome fears, phobias, and limiting beliefs is a crucial aspect of personal growth and transformation. By understanding the root causes of these emotional barriers, individuals can gain insights into their thought patterns and behaviors. NLP offers a wide array of effective strategies to address these issues, including visualization techniques, reframing negative beliefs, and anchoring positive emotions. Through visualization, individuals can mentally rehearse successful outcomes, rewiring their minds for confidence and success. Reframing, on the other hand, involves altering the perspective of a limiting belief, transforming it into a more empowering belief that aligns with personal goals.

Anchoring, another powerful NLP tool, allows individuals to associate positive emotions with a particular trigger, providing them with an emotional anchor they can access in challenging situations. By repeatedly triggering this anchor during moments of strength and confidence, individuals can create a resourceful state of mind to face fears and phobias with more resilience.

Furthermore, NLP incorporates techniques like timeline therapy, which involves revisiting past experiences that contribute to limiting beliefs or fears. Through this process, individuals can release emotional baggage and reframe past events, freeing themselves from their negative influence.

Additionally, the use of language plays a vital role in NLP. Affirmations and positive self-talk can counteract limiting beliefs and reinforce a more positive self-image. By reframing internal dialogue, individuals can change their emotional responses to past experiences, thus diminishing the hold of fears and phobias.

Guided by NLP principles, individuals can cultivate a growth mindset that encourages continuous learning and embraces challenges. Adopting a solution-oriented approach, they can transform perceived failures into valuable lessons and stepping stones toward success.

The process of overcoming fears, phobias, and limiting beliefs is a deeply personal journey, and NLP provides a versatile toolkit to navigate it effectively. By applying these strategies consistently and with determination, individuals can break free from self-imposed limitations, realize their true potential, and lead more fulfilling lives. NLP empowers individuals to take control of their emotional well-being, paving the way for growth, self-discovery, and the realization of dreams and aspirations.

•Developing a growth mindset and resilience in the face of adversity

Developing a growth mindset and resilience in the face of adversity is a fundamental aspect of personal development and success. A growth mindset is the belief that abilities and intelligence can be developed through dedication and hard work, rather than being fixed traits. Embracing a growth mindset empowers individuals to view challenges and failures as opportunities for learning and growth, rather than setbacks. It enables them to take on new challenges with enthusiasm and perseverance, knowing that effort and resilience can lead to improvement.

Resilience, on the other hand, is the ability to bounce back from difficult experiences and setbacks. It is a crucial trait that allows individuals to withstand and adapt to adversity, emerging stronger and more resourceful. NLP, with its focus on neurology, language, and behavior, offers valuable tools and techniques to foster both a growth mindset and resilience.

In NLP, individuals are encouraged to reframe their perceptions of failure and challenges. By viewing setbacks as learning experiences and opportunities for growth, they can shift their mindset and embrace challenges with a positive attitude. Visualization techniques in NLP can also play a significant role in developing resilience. By mentally rehearsing success and overcoming obstacles, individuals build confidence and inner strength, preparing them to handle adversity more effectively.

Moreover, NLP practitioners emphasize the power of language in shaping thoughts and beliefs. By using positive affirmations and self-talk, individuals can reinforce a growth mindset and resilience. They can replace self-limiting beliefs with empowering statements, fostering a more optimistic outlook on life.

Furthermore, NLP provides techniques to manage emotions effectively. Emotions like fear, self-doubt, and frustration are natural responses to adversity, but with NLP tools such as anchoring and reframing, individuals can regulate these emotions and maintain focus on their goals. Anchoring positive emotions allows individuals to access a resourceful state when faced with challenges, while reframing helps them interpret situations in a more constructive light.

In the process of developing a growth mindset and resilience, support systems and learning from role models are also vital. Engaging with like-minded individuals who share similar goals can foster encouragement and accountability. Additionally, observing successful individuals who have demonstrated resilience in the face of adversity can provide inspiration and practical insights.

By combining the principles and techniques of NLP with a strong determination to grow and thrive, individuals can cultivate a growth mindset and resilience. Embracing challenges as opportunities for growth, learning from setbacks, and maintaining a positive outlook on life are all key elements in the journey towards personal development and success. NLP equips individuals with the mindset and tools to navigate life's challenges with resilience, allowing them to flourish and achieve their aspirations.

•Empowering yourself to take control of your life and achieve success

Empowering yourself to take control of your life and achieve success is a transformative journey that requires self-awareness, determination, and the adoption of effective strategies. It involves recognizing your strengths, understanding your goals and aspirations, and developing a growth mindset that embraces challenges as opportunities for growth.

The first step towards empowerment is self-awareness. This involves gaining a deep understanding of your values, beliefs, strengths, and areas for improvement. By becoming aware of your thoughts and emotions, you can identify self-limiting beliefs and negative patterns that may be holding you back. NLP techniques such as journaling, self-reflection, and mindfulness practices can aid in developing this self-awareness.

Setting clear and meaningful goals is another essential aspect of empowerment. When you have a clear vision of what you want to achieve, it becomes easier to stay focused and motivated. NLP provides goal-setting techniques that help in creating specific, measurable, achievable, relevant, and time-bound (SMART) goals, making them more attainable and trackable.

Embracing a growth mindset is crucial for empowerment. Rather than viewing abilities and intelligence as fixed traits, a growth mindset believes that with dedication and effort, one can improve and achieve success. NLP practices like reframing negative thoughts into positive affirmations and visualizing success can reinforce this mindset, allowing you to approach challenges with resilience and determination.

Taking control of your life also involves developing effective communication and interpersonal skills. NLP offers powerful techniques for enhancing communication, understanding others' perspectives, and building rapport with people. These skills are essential for networking, building positive relationships, and collaborating with others to achieve common goals.

Overcoming fear and self-doubt is a critical aspect of empowerment. NLP provides tools for managing and transforming negative emotions, such as anchoring techniques to access resourceful states when facing challenges. By confronting fears and stepping out of your comfort zone, you can expand your horizons and realize your full potential.

Self-discipline and consistent action are key components of empowerment. NLP emphasizes the importance of taking small, manageable steps towards your goals and maintaining consistency in your efforts. This helps to build momentum and overcome obstacles along the way.

Furthermore, empowering yourself involves building a support system and seeking guidance from mentors or role models who have achieved success in areas of interest. Surrounding yourself with positive and supportive individuals can provide encouragement and motivation on your journey.

Ultimately, empowerment is about taking responsibility for your life, choices, and actions. It means acknowledging that you have the power to shape your destiny and create the life you desire. By leveraging the principles and techniques of NLP, you can cultivate the mindset, skills, and determination needed to take control of your life, overcome challenges, and achieve success in both personal and professional realms. The journey of empowerment is an ongoing process of growth and self-discovery, leading to a more fulfilling and purposeful life.

Key Takeaway

Self-Awareness: The book emphasizes the importance of self-awareness as the foundation of personal growth. Understanding your values, beliefs, strengths, and weaknesses is crucial for making positive changes in your life.

Goal Setting: Setting clear and meaningful goals using NLP's SMART techniques helps you stay focused and motivated, leading to greater chances of success.

Growth Mindset: Adopting a growth mindset enables you to view challenges as opportunities for learning and growth. This mindset helps you overcome self-limiting beliefs and approach life with resilience and determination.

Effective Communication: NLP techniques provide valuable tools for enhancing communication and building rapport with others, facilitating better relationships and collaborations.

Overcoming Fears: The book offers strategies for overcoming fears and self-doubt using anchoring techniques and positive affirmations, empowering you to face challenges with confidence.

Self-Discipline: Cultivating self-discipline and consistent action are essential for making progress towards your goals and achieving success.

Building a Support System: Surrounding yourself with positive and supportive individuals can provide encouragement and guidance on your journey to personal growth.

Taking Responsibility: Empowerment involves taking responsibility for your life and choices. By recognizing your own power to shape your destiny, you can create a fulfilling and purposeful life.

Continuous Growth: Personal growth is an ongoing process, and the book emphasizes the importance of continuous learning, improvement, and embracing new opportunities.

  By harnessing the principles and techniques of NLP, you can create a fulfilling and successful life, aligning your actions with your values and goals.

www.ingramcontent.com/pod-product-compliance
Lightning Source LLC
Chambersburg PA
CBHW061344160726
47995CB00001B/168